I Am Victorious!

Student Appreciation Techniques For Handling Conflict

(Accountable Youth Series)

I Am Victorious!

Student Appreciation Techniques For Handling Conflict

(Accountable Youth Series)

Linda M. Davis

A Critical Thinking Workbook/Portfolio

Grade 5

Students
Home Schoolers
Teachers
Parents
Counselors

Kravitz & Sons
INNOVATORS IN PUBLISHING, MARKETING AND ADVERTISING

Kravitz and Sons LLC
204 E Arlington Blvd. Suite B
Greenville, NC 27858

Published by Kravitz and Sons LLC.

ISBN: 979-8-89639-706-9 (sc)
ISBN: 979-8-89639-705-2 (e)

I can do all this through him who gives me strength (Philippians 4:13).

I Am Victorious!

Table Of Contents

Introduction

I Am Victorious is the title of the workbook/portfolio for fifth grade students, including home schoolers, from the Accountable Youth Series. It advocates experiencing a joyful life through the use of various proponents of happiness. They include learning to face problems, admitting mistakes and making the best decisions. Also, portfolios might be discussed during quarterly school conferences.

The thirty-minute weekly lessons focus on preparing children, our best gift, to rule the world one day. It champions their causes by respecting who they are individually. Through the process they learn to reach out and celebrate those in their environment. They become strengthened through a positive observable sense of self and others.

A chance is opened up to them to embrace a more purposeful life at a very young age. The lessons provided move them from thresholds of uncertainty through a garden of delightful new beginnings. Here is where they unexpectedly get to encounter rules and responsibilities as welcomed challenges in preparation for middle school.

Also, being able to smile is based on knowing what to speak, when not to speak and how to bounce back from setbacks and being scared. So, seeking harmony, overcoming fear, patience and being positive are paramount lessons that celebrate individual as well as group triumphs.

Instructions on maintaining happiness are continuous. The plan is to have happiness become contagious after enough examples of truthfulness, politeness, respect for others, problem solving and sportsmanship are witnessed.

The layout of the book includes teacher directed instructions with the word teacher written in bold print. Also, it includes key word lists, some of which are repeated for emphasis. Teachers may opt to use the current week's lesson affirmation daily. There are twenty-three affirmations.

Critical Thinking Response pages for all lessons involve students in answering questions or writing responses to statements. Content includes definitions, summaries, short stories, comparisons, notes, files, card making and teacher directed lesson preparation.

The *Accountable Youth* series works with parents and educators as they continue to seek ways to improve child rearing by working alongside students put in their care. The plan is to influence our children to affect peaceful generations of nations. Together we can explore use of positive measures as the alternative method for their accountability. Those measures include arming them with thoughts that are good, just and honest. The means we choose allows them to see us celebrate the goodness down on the inside of everyone. It's a contagious practice that is gaining momentum.

Other workbook/portfolio titles in the *Accountable Youth Series* include Caring (grade 4), *I Got This* (grade 6), *We Got This* (grade 7) and *This, This, This and That* (grade 8).

Happiness is My Choice

KEY WORD LIST:

1. happy - glad, joyful, cheerful
2. joy - a feeling of happiness, gladness, rejoicing
3. focus - become able to see clearly
4. thought - an idea or mental picture in the mind, thinking

Teachers, please copy and provide students with *your* chosen week calendar page for the following part of the lesson:

One morning some students awakened thinking about the test that they'd made a low score on the day before. Immediately each made a decision to be happy. They picked up their calendar pages and penciled in a characteristic they hoped would allow them to work on the teacher's instructions for that week. They knew that they couldn't change what happened yesterday. Their teacher had told them to think themselves happy. So, on their calendars most wrote, "I'll be happy today". Others wrote similar words. They had evidence that thinking themselves happy was encouraging them to work harder to complete their work.

Critical Thinking Response

1. Write a sentence resulting from a positive thought about yourself using either the word happy or the word joy.

_____

_____

2. Use the table of contents to list six characteristics of happy people.

_____   _____

_____   _____

_____   _____

3. Write two sentences that you can memorize to say daily before leaving home. Let them be an encouraging reminder to focus on being happy even during tough times.

a)_____

_____

b)_____

_____

I Use Positive Words

KEY WORD LIST:

1. challenge - a call to take part in a contest

2. negative - refuse to accept, deny

3. positive - acceptable, confident, sure, certain

My teacher presented a challenge to me, _____, and my classmates to begin working on using positive words. Though it might be difficult at times, we are developing positive thinking. It's beginning to show in our speech. We see our positive thoughts and words changing people's lives to make them better. So, everyday we work on having positive thoughts and words.

Critical Thinking Response

1. List two positive words that describe you.

_____

_____

2. List two positive words that might describe a relative.

_____

_____

3. Write one sentence using a positive word to say something nice about a relative who upset you even though you still love each other. Share your sentence during class time.

_____

4. In the space below illustrate an 'all occasion card' with a message to a television role model. Use the lines below to explain why you believe him or her to be a positive role model.

_____

_____

_____

_____

I Face Problems

KEY WORD LIST:

1. Problem - a thing difficult to achieve, trouble
2. Challenge - a call to take part in something possibly requiring a need for more skills
3. Solve - find an answer, settle, decide

This week I, _____, am learning more ways to face challenges and solve problems. I am looking at ways that work to solve them more quickly. Before school, at school and after school allow me chances to do this.

Critical Thinking Response

1a. Tell about a problem that any student might have before they leave home for school.

\
_____

_____

1b. Tell how to solve it quickly in a way that works.

_____

_____

2. Tell about a problem that any student might have during the school day.

_____

_____

3a. Tell about a problem that a student might have after school.

_____

_____

3b. Discuss your explanations during class time.

You have just shared problem solving in ways that could work to help yourself and others. Next time there is a problem, remember to use your problem solving skills.

I Am Happy to Admit My Mistakes

KEY WORD LIST:

1. admit - confess to be true

2. mistake - an action that is wrong, a misunderstanding

3. apology - an excuse, a statement of regret

4. idea - a thought or suggestion as a possible course of action

5. responsible - being accountable or having a duty to deal with something

This week my classmates and I are working on understanding that it's good to admit when we make mistakes. We are learning that when this happens it's always a good idea to apologize. We can ask a responsible adult for help if necessary.

Critical Thinking Response

1. Write an apology note that you believe would help schoolmates learn to say, 'I'm sorry', when mistakes are made, to three of the four people listed below:

a) parent –

_____

_____

b) another relative –

_____

_____

c) schoolmate –

_____

_____

d) teacher –

_____

_____

2. **Teachers,** give each student a large index card. Instruct them to copy the three apology notes written in number one on the card.

Students, use the copied notes as part of your personal apology reminder file. Store the card at home where you can see it and be reminded to practice saying apologies for whenever you might need to use them.

I Smile

KEY WORD LIST:

1. smile - grin, a pleased, kind facial expression usually with the corners of the mouth turned up and the front teeth showing

2. fact - truth, circumstance, information used as evidence

3. usually - regularly, in the habit of

4. naturally - in a normal manner

5. focus - become able to see clearly

I, _____, know for a fact that when I smile other people usually smile at me. Smiling naturally gives others something to smile about. Learning to focus on something as easy as smiling is lots of fun. Also, smiling encourages people to feel good about themselves during conversations. When we smile, we're happier people.

Critical Thinking Response

1. Copy the smile definition in the space below.

_____

_____

2. What thoughts go through your mind when you smile?

_____

_____

3. What thoughts go through your mind when others smile at you?

_____

_____

4. Share a conversation that you had with someone that made you smile. Use extra paper if you need it.

Title: _____

  a) First, _____

_____

  b) Next, _____

_____

  c) Then, _____

_____

  d) Finally, _____

_____

5. Why did this conversation make you smile?

_____

_____

I Try to Make the Best Decisions

KEY WORD LIST:

1. decision - the act of judging or making up one's mind, a choice

2. choice - an act of selecting or making a decision

3. affect - an emotional influence

I, _____, have been a decision maker all of my life. So, I'm getting better at learning ways I think about things so I can be safe and happy with the choices I make. Also, it's important for others. They might be affected by my decisions. I want my decisions to make them happy, too. However others might be affected by my choices and decisions I want them to be the best I can offer.

Critical Thinking Response

1. Copy the definition of decision -

_____

_____

2. I try to make the best decisions.

Draw a line from Column A to Column B to complete the sentences

Column A   Column B
If my decision is good, then my choice is _____ good
When I make a better decision, then my choice is _____ best
When I make the best decision, then my choice is _____ better

3. Copy the sentences in a, b, c, and d on the lines below each statement. My decisions will always include these four things:

a) The decisions that I make won't be based just on what I know.

_____

_____

b) My decisions will include what I want to know and need to know after talking with a responsible person.

_____

_____

c) My decisions will include what I've learned from responsible adults.

_____

_____

d) My decisions will include following directions given by those in authority over me who understand the situation.

_____

_____

I Hope for the Best

KEY WORD LIST:

1. hope - a desire for a certain thing to happen
2. challenge - a call to take part in a contest or events where extra skills are needed
3. outcome - the way something works out
4. patient - able to wait without becoming annoyed

My name is _____. My parents send me to school because they know that I will learn. They know that I will do my best to complete my school work and be obedient to those put in charge of me. My school day always involves facing challenges. However, I'm learning to be hopeful and patient while working for the best outcome.

Critical Thinking Response

1. Tell one thing that you believe most students want to happen during the school day.

_____

_____

2. Tell one thing students can do to make the above happen.

_____

_____

3. If you get off track from following the class lesson plans, tell what you could do to get back on track and continue to do your best.

_____

4. Tell one thing that you believe most students think their parents want them to do their best at when they're at home.

_____

_____

5. Tell one thing students can do to make the above happen.

_____

_____

6. Sometimes you might get off track from following your parents' plans at home. Tell about a positive way that a parent could be helpful in getting you back on track so you can get back to doing your best.

_____

_____

_____

I Follow the Rules

KEY WORD LIST:

1. follow - to go or come after
2. rules - a set of regulations to obey that govern a particular activity
3. obedience - obeying authority
4. safe – protected
5. community - all people living in a particular area
6. penalty - punishment for breaking a law

I, _____, am thankful for my parents' and teachers' rules because they teach about directions to follow. That helps me be obedient. They too must follow rules so that people in our community are safe. They must obey traffic signals when driving to prevent accidents and keep people from being hurt. This is one rule that all drivers need to follow.

Critical Thinking Response

1. Tell how following traffic signals can affect others.

_____

_____

2. Tell how not following traffic signals can affect others.

_____

_____

3. Tell about two safety rules your parents want you to follow at home and explain why.

a)

_____

_____

b)

_____

_____

4. Tell about two safety rules your teachers want you to follow during the school day and explain why.

a)

_____

_____

b)

_____

_____

5. Most students get better at following safety rules than when they were pre-schoolers. Tell about a parent or teacher safety rule that you are getting better at following than when you were much younger.

_____

_____

6. Explain how you know that your parents or teacher agree that you are better at following the safety rule above than when you were much younger.

_____

_____

I Am Responsible

KEY WORD LIST:

1. responsible - having an obligation to do something as part of a job
2. blame - hold responsible for a wrong, accuse
3. instead - as a replacement or substitute
4. detail - pay special attention to parts of a whole
5. acceptable - agreed on, satisfactory

I, _____, am a responsible person who can be counted on to follow home and school rules. Wherever I go I try to make sure that I am following my parents' and teachers' directions. If things go wrong, I work on remembering not to be angry, but take deep breaths to relax myself. This gives me a chance to cool off before trying to make any responsible decisions.

Also, I work on not blaming others. Instead, I think things out and try to come up with a plan to make things right between myself and others.

I'm thankful for being able to count on my parents and teachers to help me become more responsible at working things out.

Critical Thinking Response

1. Tell about one job responsibility around your house that your parents expect you to complete one or more times each week.

_____

_____

2. Explain what should be done for you to complete the written job responsibility in a way that is acceptable to your parents.

The steps I take to complete the job include:

a) First,

_____

_____

b) Next,

_____

_____

c) Then,

_____

_____

d) Finally,

_____

_____

I Am Helpful

KEY WORD LIST:

1. help - make it easier to do something by providing support or assistance
2. ask - say something in order to obtain an answer or information
3. superhero - a pretend being with extraordinary powers who uses them to protect the innocent

I, _____, am remembering that when schoolmates need help they may choose to ask me for it. Asking for help means questioning somebody. It means speaking in a friendly voice. When they speak that way I will be more comfortable around them when they ask for help.

I, too, can ask a responsible person for help. Also, if I see others who are in trouble I can make a decision to help or get the help of a responsible adult.

Critical Thinking Response

1. Explain what kind of help might be given by a positive superhero or role model on a favorite television show or video.

_____

_____

_____

2. Tell about a time when you were a positive role model for a student of any age.

_____

_____

3. Invent a new positive superhero who is a role model for students. Write a paragraph that best describes them as being someone who helps kids. Explain how they'd be helpful as a role model.

Name of superhero role model:

_____

_____

_____

_____

4. **Teachers,** give directions for your students to use lined paper to work in small groups writing short plays asking someone for help. Allow time for them to practice and perform in class in the next two to three days.

Title of short play: _____

Student Authors: _____   _____

Characters: _____   _____

_____   _____

_____   _____

Story Location: _____

I Bounce Back from Setbacks and Feeling Scared

KEY WORD LIST:

1. setback - a change from better to worse
2. scared - fearful, afraid
3. important - of great value
4. troublesome - bothersome, difficult
5. summary - a short account of the main points of something

I, _____, go to my parents or other responsible people for help when I'm feeling sad, upset or troubled about anything. They teach me that it's very important to find something good to think about or do whenever I'm sad or during other troublesome times. It helps me get back on the right track so that I can work on being happier. Being happy helps repair hurt feelings. Sometimes setbacks happen, but with help I bounce back from them.

Also, whenever I'm scared, I share my fears with my parents or other responsible adults. We talk things over until I feel better. They encourage me to think positive and happy thoughts. This helps me bounce back from scared feelings.

Critical Thinking Response

1. What happened to help you bounce back from one particular setback or a time that you felt scared?

_____

_____

2. **Teachers,** allow your students to share their *bounce back* stories.

3. Use **teacher** selected literature to explain thoughts, ideas or facts that a story character used to help him or her bounce back from a troublesome situation.

Title: _____

Character: _____

a) Describe the troublesome time that the person was having.

_____

_____

_____

b) What positive thoughts helped this person move from being sad, upset or scared so they could bounce back from the setback that they'd experienced?

_____

_____

_____

c) What action was taken that helped with bouncing back from a setback?

_____

_____

_____

I Am a Positive Person

KEY WORD LIST:

1. positive - sure, certain, acceptable, confident

2. negative - refusal to accept, denial

3. task - job, duty, work

4. attitude - a settled way of thinking or feeling reflected in one's behavior

5. courteous - polite, respectful

I, _____, am learning to take control over negative thoughts by thinking positive thoughts. So, I think about things that are good. Sometimes negative thoughts happen when things aren't going my way. When this happens it's a signal to my brain to bounce back to good thoughts. Good thoughts make me feel happy. They return my positive thinking. They help me have respect for myself and a better attitude towards others. Also, my positive attitude causes others to have a better attitude towards me.

Critical Thinking Response

1. **Teacher** chosen literature title –

_____

_____

2. Copy a story sentence that lets you know that negative thinking was happening.

_____

_____

3. Was there a story character who tried to replace negative thinking with positive thinking?

_____

_____

4. Tell who was helpful and how in leading the story character to positive thinking.

_____

_____

5. What happened when positive thinking took place?

_____

_____

6. Pretend that a sister or brother burst into your room forgetting to be courteous by knocking. Write a positive message you could use the next time this happens.

_____

_____

7. Forgive others even when it is difficult to do so. Sometimes it takes a while to forgive. The sooner we do so, that's when we begin to feel powerful again.

Sometimes we need others to forgive us of wrongs we do to them. Write a short paragraph telling what you'd want to hear from someone who forgives you.

_____

I Seek Harmony

KEY WORD LIST:

1. seek - attempt to find, search, look for
2. harmony - in agreement, unity
3. respect - admire, esteem, honor
4. often - many times, frequently
5. agreement - harmony in opinion or feeling

I, _____, work at being in agreement with others to prevent them and myself from being upset or angry. This is necessary because it helps me treat others with respect. When they feel respected, they often agree with me because they know that I'm trying to be friendly. Then, each of us is happy. This kind of agreement is called harmony.

I seek harmony in my home, in my classroom and on the playground with adults and children.

Critical Thinking Response

1. Write a pretend conversation in which you were seeking harmony with someone on the playground.

_____

_____

2. What makes you think the conversation ended with both of you being in agreement?

_____

_____

3. Tell about a positive harmonious event that involved people living in your house.

_____

_____

4. What thoughts might have gone through your mind to keep you on track so that you could be in agreement with others involved in the event?

_____

_____

5. Tell about a positive harmonious event involving students and teachers that happened at your school last year or this year.

_____

_____

6. What thoughts might have gone through your mind to keep you on track so that you could be in agreement with other students and teachers involved in the event?

_____

_____

I Am Kind

KEY WORD LIST:

1. kind - nice, good, gentle
2. focus - the center of interest or activity
3. sibling - a brother or sister
4. relative - a person connected by blood or marriage
5. treat - to act or behave toward a person in some specified way

I, _____, am kind. I'm working on being kinder to my parents, relatives, school mates and everybody that I meet. When I speak to them I focus on treating them the way I want to be treated. When I offer to help others they seem happy and thankful even when they don't need the help. The kindness that I give out is not always returned by them, but sometimes by others instead.

Critical Thinking Response

1. Tell about a kind act for someone at home that a student could do that isn't a responsibility given by a parent.

_____

_____

2. Tell about a kind act that you could do around your house with a parent's permission.

_____

_____

3. Pretend that you overheard some kids calling another kid bad names. Write something you could say that would make the kid feel better.

_____

_____

4. Pretend that a new student has arrived in your classroom and is sitting alone during recess because no one has asked him or her to join a group activity. Write something you could say to that student which would encourage her or him to join your group.

_____

_____

5. Pretend that someone starts gossiping about another kid at school whom you might not know. Write something you could say to the gossiper so that they'll know that gossip is hurtful and wrong. You can use these words even if a friend is gossiping.

_____

_____

I Am Polite

KEY WORD LIST:

1. polite - having or showing respectful and considerate behavior
2. please - used as a polite addition to requests
3. thank you - a polite expression used when receiving a gift, service, compliment, or accepting or refusing an offer
4. phrase - two or more words arranged to act as part of a sentence
5. permission - permitting or giving authority
6. respect - admire, esteem, honor
7. authority - the power or right to give orders and enforce obedience

I, _____, am polite. Today I'm learning more about how to be polite to others. I'm learning from my parents and teachers. Polite words and phrases that they use include please, thank you and may I. I can tell that people feel good about themselves when I, too, say please, thank you or may I. So, I'll set an example for others to follow by continuing to use these words.

Critical Thinking Response

1. During the next school day, observe reasons that you hear people giving for saying polite words and phrases. When you return to class list and share two of those reasons below:

a)

_____

_____

b)

_____

_____

31

2. Tell about a time that you were polite to someone and used the words *please* and/or *thank you.*

_____

_____

3. Tell about a time that someone was polite to you and used the words *please* and/or *thank you.*

_____

_____

4. How did you feel when they used polite words?

_____

5. The phrase *May I* is used when you are seeking someone's permission to use something. Pretend that you might need permission to use something that belongs to someone else. Write a note, using the phrase *May I,* that could be used as a reminder of a polite way to ask their permission to do so.

_____

_____

6. You might want to go somewhere but need permission from someone in authority. Write a note, using the phrase *May I,* as a reminder of a polite way to get their permission. However, keep in mind that a person in authority uses their best judgment when it comes to making the best decisions, even when you're polite.

_____

_____

I Like Who I Am

KEY WORD LIST:

focus - to concentrate on something specific, see it more clearly

I, _____, like who I am and who I am becoming. I have people who take care of me. They encourage me to focus on being my best self. They say that I can do this by focusing on thinking and acting responsibly. That's how I can increase the goodness others see and become my best self.

Critical Thinking Response

1. Use the *Table of Contents* to list characteristics on the short line which best describe you. On the long line, explain why you believe your description of yourself (because...).

I know that... because...

a) I am _____

_____

b) I am _____

_____

c) I am _____

_____

d) I am _____

_____

e) I am _____

_____

f) I am _____

_____

g) I am _____

_____

h) I am _____

_____

i) I am _____

_____

j) I am _____

_____

2. List two main characteristics in this lesson that you are working on:

a)_____ b) _____

3. Tell what you're doing at home to be more like one of the above characteristics.

_____

_____

4. Explain what you could focus on doing using that characteristic if you ride the school bus or eat in the school cafeteria.

_____

_____

5. Tell what you're doing in the classroom to be more like the other listed characteristic.

_____

_____

6. Tell what you could do to focus on that second characteristic during recess time or gym class.

_____

_____

I Am A Good Sport

KEY WORD LIST:

1. good sport - a person who plays fair, accepts both victory and defeat
2. sportsmanship - treating the team you play against as you'd like to be treated
3. attitude - a settled way of thinking or feeling
4. challenge - a call to take part in a contest
5. hero - one who is admired for courage or noble qualities, a role model

I, _____, enjoy activities that involve fast thinking and movement. Some things that some of my classmates and I like include exercise, dancing, sports and some board games. We like challenges. We have many at school that give us many chances to get better at being good sportsmen.

We are working on qualities for becoming *good sports*. We're learning by frequently practicing saying the words:

1. I am a good sport because I stay in the game.
2. No matter the score, all who stay in the game are winners.
3. All who do their best are winners.
4. All who have a good attitude are winners. It's all part of good sportsmanship.

Critical Thinking Response

1. Tell about the positive behavioral skills of a favorite sports hero or television character. You may choose to use qualities listed in the table of contents as well as other behaviors.

_____

_____

2. Tell what happened when he or she showed good sportsmanship.

_____

_____

3. Complete the sentences below from this lesson. They will help you explain to others the requirements of good sportsmanship.

a) I'm working on becoming a good sportsman by

_____

_____

b) No matter what the score is,

_____

_____

c) All who do their best

_____

_____

d) All who have a

_____

_____

4. **Teachers,** remind students of the importance of encouraging themselves to do their best. By frequently practicing reading the qualities of a good sportsman they are encouraging themselves to improve their skills.

Teachers, allow students to pair up and take turns reading and pretending to work with a classmate who didn't feel like being a good sport when others were cheered for instead of her or him.

5. This week practice good sportsmanship at home or at school using one of the choices below:

- Challenge someone by playing a board game
- Challenge someone with a foot race
- Challenge someone with another skill that everyone agrees on

6. Tell how you 'kept your cool', even if others didn't.

_____

_____

I Practice Saying Good Things

KEY WORD LIST:

1. negative - refusal to accept, denial
2. mean - unwilling to share things
3. practice - a habit of using an idea or method
4. gossip - to spread rumors or talk about someone that is personal
5. human - characteristic of people

I, _____, and my classmates are learning to speak words that help others feel good about themselves. The good words that we speak encourage them to want to increase their abilities.

Whenever I hear something negative or bad about a person, I remind myself to replace it with a good thought. Whenever I hear someone calling another person a bad name I replace it with a good word or name. Whenever I do this, it gives me more practice saying what is good. The more often I say good things, the easier it becomes to think good thoughts.

When we join others who say good things about a person, it builds that person up. Then, they can do more good things in life and be happier, too. Also, they, too, learn to speak good words about others because of the examples we set for them.

We can practice speaking good words by:

1. Making a decision to change our thinking so that when bad thoughts cross our minds, we immediately replace them with good thoughts
2. Controlling our mouths so that we don't speak negative words

Critical Thinking Response

1. On the lines below, write some of your good characteristics that you might use on a *Thinking of Me* card.

_____   _____

_____   _____

_____   _____

2. On a separate piece of paper illustrate a *Thinking of Me* card for yourself. Include words that replace negative speaking by yourself or others. Make sure that it's one that you can use to remind yourself to read if mean words or gossip are said about you.

3. Use paper to illustrate a *Thinking of You* card for a parent or a caregiver.

I Respect Others

KEY WORD LIST:

1. respect - admire, esteem, honor

2. treatment - action or behavior toward a person

3. worthy - having worth, value, honor

4. obedient - obeying instructions of one in authority

5. summary - an account of the main points of something

I, _____, respect my parents, teachers and schoolmates. I respect those put in authority over me. Respect is the kind of treatment that every human is worthy of having. All people are able to show respect. Respect can be shown in many positive ways. I show it by being friendly, obedient and listening.

Critical Thinking Response

1. Give an example of a way you can show respect by being friendly to a new schoolmate?

_____

_____

2. Give an example of a way you can show respect by being obedient to an older student given authority by an adult over you.

_____

_____

3. Pretend that a student is standing before your class giving a speech. Think about how to focus your attention skills on what he or she is saying. Then, write

two sentences that would encourage the speaker to believe that you're listening to what they're saying.

a)

_____

_____

b)

_____

_____

4. To check your listening skills, write a summary for a positive children's movie. It should be one that parents or teachers allowed you to watch because of the respect shown by a responsible role model.

Title:_____

_____

_____

_____

_____

_____

_____

I Am Truthful

KEY WORD LIST:

1. truth - reality, fact

2. afraid - feeling fear or anxiety, scared

3. lie - an intentionally false statement

4. upset - to make unhappy, to cause disorder, disappointment

5. situation - a set of circumstances in which one finds oneself

6. patch - repair, fix or strengthen a torn or weak point

7. serious - demanding careful consideration, important

I, _____, will remember to tell the truth because my parents and teachers say it's the best way to fix my problems.

Whenever I feel afraid to be truthful, I remember that telling a lie makes a situation worse than telling the truth even if it upsets you and I. It takes longer to fix a lie and then get to the truth. After telling the truth, with someone's help, you might be able to patch things up. With help, you could make room for new plans and more caring friendships. It is never acceptable to tell a lie.

Critical Thinking Response

1. Use a story about a hero or television actor telling about a truth that was held back.

_____

_____

2. How was the truth revealed?

_____

3. Tell how the problem could have been fixed sooner.

_____

_____

4. Lying is unacceptable and irresponsible behavior. Pretend that you are a television hero or actor who strongly believes in telling the truth. Write a three to five sentence paragraph which that person might use to convince others of the seriousness of telling a lie instead of being truthful.

_____

_____

_____

_____

_____

I Am a Peacemaker

KEY WORD LIST:

1. peacemaker - one who settles disputes, makes peace
2. prevent - to keep something from happening
3. apologize - offer an excuse for some fault, failure or injury
4. solution - a means of solving a problem, an answer
5. threaten - state one's intention to take harmful action against someone
6. unforgiveness - a grudge against someone who has offended you
7. forgiveness - to excuse for a fault or an offense

I, _____, am a peacemaker. I continue to be in training to be the best peacemaker that I can be. This means that I:

- Work on both home rules and school responsibilities
- Use a loud voice only on the playground unless needed or permitted, in other places, by those in authority
- Make new friends and try to keep the old responsible ones
- Help prevent arguments by staying out of negative conversations
- Help find solutions to problems by using a positive attitude to discuss them
- Apologize when others feel threatened by me
- Forgive negative words and actions because it hurts if I hold on to them
- Try to help others understand when they misunderstand what I'm saying

As a peacemaker, I forgive so that unforgiveness won't control me and take away from my happiness. Then, after a while I truly feel and know that I've forgiven others. It's very important to forgive because it helps us become better peacemakers.

Critical Thinking Response

1. Copy the peacemaker definition from the key word list.

_____

_____

Teachers, start a classroom *apology card file* that uses positive words and phrases. The file should include the first and last name of the contributing student. Students can use the file to help those feeling offended, those who want to become better peacemakers and those who are already peacemakers.

Use the space below to design an apology card for the file. This can be done by including some of the words found in the key word list of this and other lessons.

This page will serve as the practice page for your apology card. After your teacher sees it, copy the same information with your first and last name on a large index card. Then, put it in a box that your teacher will label with the words *Peacemaker* Box. The cards won't need illustrations.

I Celebrate Others' Triumphs

KEY WORD LIST:

1. celebrate - to do something enjoyable to mark a happy event
2. jealousy - envy against another's success or happiness
3. envious - feeling jealous of another's success or happiness
4. triumph - a great victory or achievement
5. cheer - shout for joy and in praise or encouragement
6. uncomfortable - causing an uneasy or distressful feeling

I, _____, am so excited about telling my friends my good news! I know they'll be happy for me. I've already celebrated at home by jumping up and down and spinning round and round. Others in my house joined in the fun and we had a great time. Our talking and laughing encouraged all of us until late in the evening.

At our house we celebrate everybody's good news. It's important to celebrate with those who are experiencing feelings of triumphs. We cheer for them the way we want them to cheer for us when our turn comes to celebrate. Sometimes people are jealous if good news isn't happening to them when it happens to you. Also, maybe they're envious if they believe your reason for being triumphant is better than theirs. They should not compare their lives to yours. When this happens, it makes others around them feel uncomfortable.

Remember to share your good news with people who celebrate your triumphs by smiling and speaking words that cheer you up.

Remember to encourage the good works of friends and of those who are jealous. By doing this you are setting a good example for others to follow. Look for small ways to encourage others. Your attitude about celebrating others will help cure jealousy.

Critical Thinking Response

1. Tell about a time that someone celebrated your good news.

_____

_____

_____

_____

_____

_____

2. Tell about a time that you celebrated somebody else's good news.

_____

_____

_____

_____

_____

_____

We Are Victorious!

KEY WORD LIST:

1. joyful - feeling or causing happiness
2. victorious - having won a victory
3. successful - having achieved honor, wealth, position, fortunate
4. communicate - to share or exchange information, news, ideas
5. practice - the use of an idea, belief or method
6. method - a way of doing something
7. agreement - harmony in opinion or feeling

I, _____, am a joyful person! It's because I worked hard to successfully follow all of the directions in this workbook. Also, to help me be victorious in other places, I took part in positive activities away from school.

With my parents' and teachers' help I will continue to learn about communicating with others and being victorious.

Schoolmates helped me learn how to treat them. We worked together by practicing positive thinking. It led to positive speaking that encouraged everyone to feel victorious most often. We learned that we should practice being joyful everyday because it makes us feel victorious. Through practice, I found this teaching to be true.

We worked individually and as a group to make a great difference in learning how to care for and celebrate ourselves and others. We can use these joyful methods for being victorious all of our lives!

Critical Thinking Response

1. Tell about a positive situation that happened this year that made you feel victorious.

_____

_____

_____

2. This workbook involved the whole class being in agreement with learning more about being joyful and victorious people. List the first names of the others in this class who completed the work in this book and share your victory.

_____ _____ _____ _____

_____ _____ _____ _____

_____ _____ _____ _____

_____ _____ _____ _____

Teacher's Signature: _____

3. **Teachers,** please provide an award certificate for each student completing this workbook.